RACING LEGENDS

LEWIS HAMILTON

100% UNOFFICIAL

Published 2024 by Macmillan Children's Books
an imprint of Pan Macmillan
The Smithson, 6 Briset Street, London EC1M 5NR
EU representative: Macmillan Publishers Ireland Ltd, 1st Floor,
The Liffey Trust Centre, 117–126 Sheriff Street Upper
Dublin 1, D01 YC43
Associated companies throughout the world
www.panmacmillan.com

ISBN 978-1-0350-3513-7

3 5 7 9 8 6 4 2

A CIP catalogue record for this book is available from the British Library.

Printed and bound by CPI Group (UK) Ltd, Croydon CR0 4YY

MIX
Paper | Supporting responsible forestry
FSC® C116313
FSC www.fsc.org

All facts correct at time of printing.

RACING LEGENDS

LEWIS HAMILTON

Maurice Hamilton

Illustrated by Cat Sims

MACMILLAN CHILDREN'S BOOKS

CONTENTS

Formula 1 is one of the **most exciting** sports in the world.

It is **noisy, colourful** – and VERY, VERY **FAST!**

Formula 1 cars can reach speeds of up to **320 kmh (200 mph).** That's three times faster than the 113-kmh (70-mph) speed limit on motorways, the fastest roads you can use in the UK.

The F1 cars race side-by-side at these **unbelievable speeds.**

It takes very special and very **brave drivers** to do this in these **incredible** machines.

That's why the twenty F1 drivers are the **best in the world**. They come from all sorts of countries, and race all around the globe.

I love watching F1. I've been SO lucky to attend more than 500 Grands Prix around the world!

These drivers compete against each other in races known as **Grands Prix** (which means 'Great Prize' in French!).

And it certainly is a Great Prize – champion teams win millions of pounds!

They drive for ten F1 teams, with two drivers in each of these **top teams.**

Ferrari is the most famous. The Italian team has been racing **for more than 75 years.**

The Mercedes and Red Bull teams have won the most races in the past 10 years. Both these teams are based in England.

There are more that twenty Grands Prix held from March to November around the world.

Each racetrack is different. Some are on city streets – like in Monte Carlo, Baku in Azerbaijan or Las Vegas in the United States. Once the Grand Prix has finished, the crash barriers and grandstands are removed and the normal traffic – cars, buses, vans – returns to the streets.

Other Grands Prix are on permanent circuits built for racing – like Silverstone in England, Suzuka in Japan or Monza in Italy.

The length of the laps is also different. Monaco is the shortest at 3.34 km (2.07 miles). Spa in Belgium is the longest at 7 km (4.35 miles).

Each race lasts for an hour and a half – sometimes longer.

The winner of each race receives twenty-five championship points. Points are awarded down to 10th place like this:

1st : 25
2nd : 18
3rd : 15
4th : 12
5th : 10
6th : 8
7th : 6
8th : 4
9th : 2
10th : 1

After the last race of the year, the driver with the most points becomes **World Champion!**

This is the greatest honour in motor racing. The World Champion is the BEST driver.

There have been thirty-four different World Champions in the past 74 years.

Some drivers have become World Champion more than once.

But only two drivers in F1 history have been World Champions **SEVEN times . . .**

And there's only **ONE driver in the WORLD** who has won **more than 100 Grands Prix . . .**

. . . He is the **ultimate Racing Legend . . .**

LEWIS HAMILTON!

WHO IS LEWIS HAMILTON?

Lewis Hamilton is one of the world's best-known sportsmen.

He is the only Black champion in F1 and he is known for helping to make the world a better place, beyond the racetrack.

Without a doubt, Lewis Hamilton is **the most successful F1 driver – EVER!**

Did you know, that so far, the English driver has won **103 Grands Prix?**

That's a MASSIVE number of wins. One other legend, Michael Schumacher, won ninety-one Grands Prix. But Lewis soon overtook him!

No other driver racing today comes close to

Lewis's number of Grands Prix wins.

Of the twenty drivers racing in F1 now, Max Verstappen has won less than 50 GPs. Fernando Alonso has won thirty-two. The rest are much further behind.

Lewis Hamilton has won **seven World Championships.** Max Verstappen has won three. Fernando Alonso has won two.

Lewis Hamilton has been racing in F1 since 2007. He has driven for McLaren and, since 2013, Mercedes.

Lewis has started from pole position an amazing **104 times** and has **finished in the top three more times than any other driver.** He has stood on the podium and sprayed champagne more than **195 times.** That's an incredible amount of spray!

He has **led more than 5000 laps.** That equals roughly 27,678 km (17,000 miles). That's three-quarters of the way around the earth! Or twenty-eight times up and down Great Britain from Land's End at the tip of Cornwall to John O'Groats at the top of Scotland.

Lewis uses his success and fame to set new boundaries in sport and in life.

He has campaigned against racism and encourages diversity in motor racing and all sports.

Lewis launched his charitable foundation 'Mission 44' to empower young people from underserved groups. He encourages them to succeed, not just in motor racing, but in anything they do.

Lewis also has interests in music and fashion. He uses his own story as a shining example of what can be achieved when you work hard towards your goals.

Time magazine listed Lewis Hamilton as **one of the 100 most influential people in**

the whole world! This includes scientists, presidents, politicians, artists and other brilliant people.

Lewis had what he describes as 'a very ordinary upbringing' on a council estate in Stevenage, to the north of London. Lewis went on to become a champion in every level of motor racing on his way to being recognised as one of the greatest drivers of all time. But he never forgot his roots.

Lewis began racing at the age of eight and is **still competing more than 30 years later.**

In 2020, he was knighted by Prince Charles at Windsor Castle and became Sir Lewis Hamilton.

While growing up in Stevenage, Lewis never believed he could have achieved such a fantastic honour. But that did not stop him from wanting to be the very best in everything he did.

LEWIS'S LEGENDARY STATS

Coordination:	**10/10**
Control:	**9/10**
Precision:	**7/10**
Balance:	**10/10**
Wet Weather Skills:	**10/10**

Acceleration:	**8/10**
Fitness:	**8/10**
Staying calm:	**9/10**
Split-second decisions:	**9/10**
Strategy:	**7/10**

Lewis Hamilton is a very, very fast driver. There are many reasons for this.

From the moment Lewis began playing with a remote-controlled car at the age of six, Anthony Hamilton noticed his son's incredible hand-to-eye **co-ordination.** It was easy for Lewis to control exactly where the car went. This came naturally to him.

Lewis would get better and better as he began kart racing and moved into racing cars. He could position the car perfectly going through a corner and could cope with whatever happened. He was not afraid of the car thanks to being able to make it do exactly what he wanted. He was always in **control.**

There were no wild movements as he steered the car with perfect **precision.**

Lewis has a great sense of **balance.** He can feel the car through his body. He knows just how fast he can go through a corner without losing control and spinning off.

This is really important when it's raining, and the racetrack becomes slippery. Lewis's **wet weather skills** are the best in Grand Prix racing as he somehow manages to go faster than everyone else without sliding off the track.

Lewis is extremely **fit.** He can drive very fast for long periods of time without becoming tired or losing concentration.

He remains **calm,** despite having to race at speeds of up to 320 kmh (200 mph) with other cars very close to his. By staying calm, he can make **split-second decisions** and work out the best place to overtake the driver in front.

Grand Prix races are 300 km (190 miles) long. Lewis is very good at looking after his car –

even while driving flat out – and making sure the tyres and brakes have not worn out before the finish.

He works with his engineer to devise the best **strategy** for each race. This is when he decides the time is right to go really fast and attack other drivers. And when he can back off to save his tyres and the car.

After each race, he can sit down with his engineer and describe exactly what the car was doing – where it was good and where it was bad – in order to make it better for the next race. This is typical of Lewis **never giving up and wanting to be the BEST!**

LEWIS'S FAMILY

In 1955, Lewis Hamilton's grandfather moved from Grenada in the West Indies to seek a better life in England.

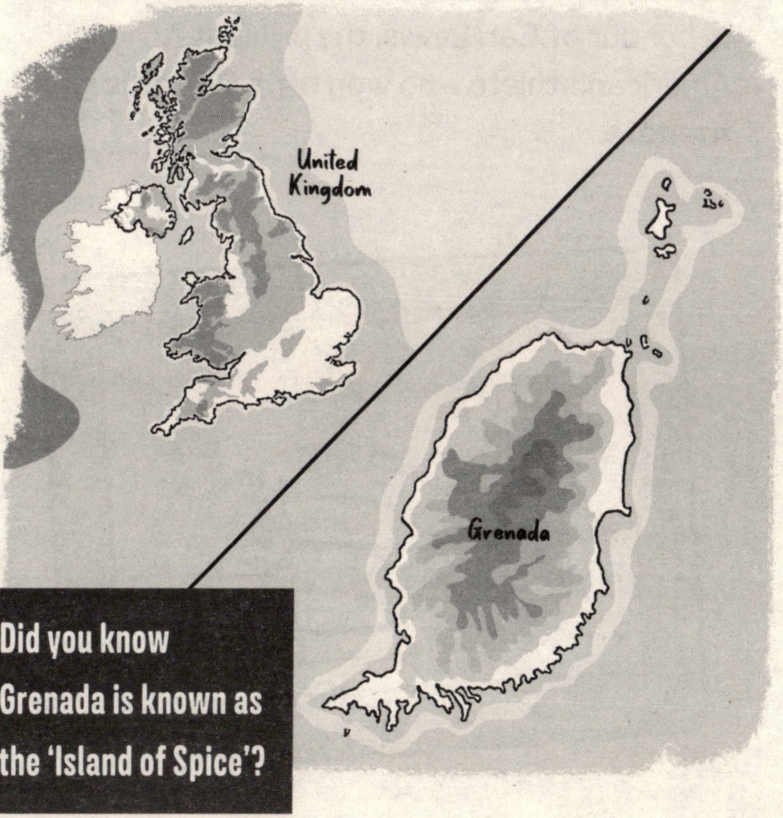

Did you know Grenada is known as the 'Island of Spice'?

Lewis's father, Anthony, was born in 1963 and the Hamilton family moved from West London to Stevenage, which was then a new town in Hertfordshire.

When Lewis was born on 7 January 1985, he was given the middle name 'Carl'. It was his father's middle name, but it was also chosen in honour of Carl Lewis, the brilliant African American athlete who won **nine Olympic gold medals.**

Lewis was described by his schoolteacher as a 'bright, smiley, happy boy'.

Carl Lewis won 65 long jump tournaments in a row over a span of 10 years. That's legendary!

When he was bullied at school, Lewis kept smiling and took up karate to build up his self-confidence. Karate teaches discipline, self-control and poise, all skills Lewis would later use in his driving. He became a Black Belt – the top level in karate – at the age of just twelve!

It was a sign of his burning ambition to be the best at whatever he did and not be put off by anything.

REMOTE-CONTROLLED RACING

After seeing just how good Lewis was at operating a remote-controlled car at the age of six, Anthony took Lewis to a radio-controlled car club run by a model shop in Stevenage.

This was a serious hobby for many grown-ups. They carefully built and raced model cars

using hand-held controls. These races were held on miniature racetracks which were very tricky with lots of bends, curves and flyovers.

These cars were much faster than the battery car Lewis had used when playing at home. And yet he found it easy to operate the hand-held controls that worked these sophisticated little racing machines.

He was so fast that he became the champion – beating grown-ups from all the local model car clubs! It was an amazing sight; the bright-eyed and focussed boy standing among all the adults and blowing them away on this mini racetrack. This had never happened before! Everyone was amazed.

A few years before, while on holiday in Spain, Lewis and his Dad had visited a track with electric karts for kids. It was a very small track, with only a couple of corners. Anthony had wanted to see how Lewis got on, even though he could barely reach the pedals!

Lewis loved being able to control the kart, making it go fast and taking the corners as quickly as he could. He was only six at the time, but imagined he was **Ayrton Senna**, the World Champion with McLaren, racing at Silverstone or Monaco.

Ayrton Senna was a Brazilian F1 superstar. From 1989 to 2006 he held the record for most pole positions. He is one of Lewis's big inspirations.

ZOOOOOM!

He'd never gone so fast in his life.

Driving a kart gave him such a thrill – better than anything else he had ever experienced. He loved playing cricket and football (Lewis supports Arsenal!) and enjoyed all sorts of competitive sports at school.

But this was different.

He came to realize this was what he wanted to do more than anything else in the world.

He wanted to drive.

A QUICK GUIDE TO KART RACING

Karting (or Go-Karting) is the first stepping-stone to becoming a serious racing driver.

Karts are mini racing cars. They are made with a metal frame and little wheels, powered by a small engine – like the motor in a lawn mower. There are just two pedals and a steering wheel. The pedal on the right – the accelerator – makes the kart GO! The pedal on the left – the brake – slows it down. That's it!

The smallest karts for the youngest drivers – aged five or six – can have bumpers all the way round. That way it doesn't matter if you hit anything – although that's not encouraged! These karts are for fun driving and not for racing.

Kart racing is divided into categories, depending on your age.

These are the classes and ages:

Bambino	6-8
Cadet	8-12
Inter	10-13
Junior	12-16
Senior	15+

Which category would you race in?

There is another class for senior drivers in karts with gearboxes – but that's for later! The smaller karts just go when you put your right foot on the accelerator (or throttle), and slow when you use your left foot on the brake pedal. All you have to do after that is steer. Simple!

Some of the smallest karts have electric engines. These karts can be driven on indoor tracks.

The karting experience begins with the **Bambino** class. Bambinos do not race. Instead, they have time trials where the karts set off at various intervals and the laps are timed. At some tracks, the drivers can be graded into Gold, Silver and Bronze categories depending on how fast they go. Their record cards are updated as they improve and go faster.

The races for **Cadets** are held on short and small tracks, specially built for karting. The older you get, the longer the circuits become – and the faster you go!

Most kart events have qualifying sessions, with the fastest driver going to the front of the starting grid and the slowest at the back – just like at a Grand Prix!

If there are lots of drivers, the entry will be split into heats, with the winner of each heat going into a Final. That's when the racing gets really close and exciting!

Once kart drivers begin racing, they must wear proper overalls, gloves, boots and a crash helmet – the same type of equipment used by every Grand Prix driver. The majority of Grand Prix drivers began their racing careers in karts.

Each kart driver begins racing in their own country. Once they become the best at home, they race in Europe against the best from other countries and, in many cases, go on to compete in the World Championships to determine who is the VERY BEST kart racer in the world.

Many great Grand Prix drivers from the past – Ayrton **Senna,** Alain **Prost,** Nico **Rosberg,** Michael **Schumacher** – started in karting.

And so did Lewis **Hamilton.**

LEWIS GOES KARTING!

Once Lewis was old enough to race at the age of eight, his father bought a second-hand kart and entered Lewis at a local kart race.

They chose the **number 44** for the kart – it was on the number plate of his dad's Vauxhall road car and Lewis would continue to use it where possible throughout his racing career.

From Karting and F1 to Lewis's charity, Mission 44, it's clear that 44 is Lewis's lucky number! Do you have a favourite number?

Lewis was immediately very fast. When starting off in karting, novice drivers have their numbers on a black plate for the first six races so that you can spot them easily on the track. Once they have progressed to the next level, their numbers are put on yellow plates.

When Lewis started as a novice, he was not only the fastest of the black plates at virtually every race, but he was racing in among the yellow plates! This caught the attention of established kart racers.

The experts were impressed by the young novice in kart number 44 racing as he beat older and more experienced drivers. It was just like how he'd beaten much more experienced players in remote-controlled car racing!

Lewis appeared to be doing all this without any effort or drama. He was very fast and he smiled through each race. The first step in becoming the best at something is enjoying it!

Lewis's father didn't have lots of money and karting can be an expensive sport. But Lewis was so good that, by the age of ten, he was receiving sponsorship from karting experts who helped to pay for tyres and look after his kart, just to make sure Lewis could keep racing.

And it quickly paid off for them.

Lewis became the **youngest driver ever to win the British Cadet Karting Championship.**

He received his trophy at the prestigious Autosport Awards in a fancy London hotel. This annual ceremony honoured the top racing drivers in the world; all the very important people from motor racing were present.

After he had received his award, Lewis walked up to the McLaren table of guests and introduced himself to Ron Dennis, the boss of the famous racing team. Lewis told Mr Dennis that he one day wanted to be World Champion in one of his McLaren Grand Prix cars. They talked for 10 minutes. Mr Dennis was impressed by the calm confidence of this young man who could barely see over the table. He told Lewis to call him in 9 years and they would sort something out.

Mr Dennis would want to get in touch much sooner than that – thanks to the fantastic progress being made by Lewis in the junior categories of motor racing.

Lewis continued to win championships in junior karting. At each level, the karts were more powerful and faster. Lewis mastered them all. He was ready to keep moving up. But this was going to cost money Lewis and his family didn't have. Luckily, he'd caught the eye of McLaren-Mercedes's Ron Dennis, who knew he needed to help support Lewis's development. McLaren would provide financial support and keep an eye on Lewis's progress.

McLaren are one of the oldest teams in F1. Their cars have been in every year of competition since 1966!

Instead of taking the kart to races in a battered trailer towed by Anthony's old Vauxhall, they were given a brand-new Mercedes van and Mercedes car.

A wide-eyed thirteen-year-old Lewis was among six young kart drivers at the launch of the McLaren-Mercedes support scheme. He got to see the massive McLaren factory in Woking with its great F1 cars from the past.

Lewis also got to meet McLaren's F1 drivers, **Mika Häkkinen** and **David Coulthard.**

Mika Häkkinen would become World Champion for McLaren in that year (1998) and the year after!

Lewis was impressed and inspired by McLaren's cabinets full of silver trophies – there were hundreds of them!

He wanted to add trophies of his own to this

collection. He was determined to become a Grand Prix champion for McLaren. He now believed it was possible.

But first, he had to win more races and championships to prove to Ron Dennis that he was worth supporting. McLaren were not only providing money, but also technical support and professional advice. But they wouldn't do all that if the young driver was not winning.

Lewis found himself racing in the next class of karting against teenagers several years older than he was. These fifteen- and sixteen-year-olds were more experienced, bigger and physically stronger. They were the same kart racers he had looked up to when he was a junior. Now he was racing against them. That was a big deal!

But Lewis did not allow himself to worry. He just focussed totally on driving the kart. He thought of nothing else. The first race of the season would provide a huge test.

It was time to prove himself.

The first race of the karting season was held near Glasgow in Scotland, far away from Lewis's home. The race was held in pouring rain. He zipped and darted left and right on the wet surface – he had to get in front of two of the older racers.

Steering is much more difficult in the rain. Driving at high speeds on wet surfaces can be dangerous and requires very skilled drivers.

One of them spun off while trying to keep Lewis behind in third place. Lewis then sped ahead and caught up with the leader. He challenged him hard. And, **never giving up,** he found a way into the lead! The rain fell even heavier. And Lewis pulled away, extended his lead to a **massive** 15 seconds – and scored a brilliant **victory!**

The next races were held in dry conditions. Lewis found it tough to beat the more experienced drivers. But he hung in there! He built up his speed, learning new tricks as he went.

In the second half of the season, he was a serious contender for wins. By the time the championship reached the final race, Lewis was neck and neck with Fraser Sheader for the title – the driver he had beaten in that first race in Scotland!

Lewis won the final race – but Sheader became champion because he had scored more points during the season. It was so close!

McLaren were impressed by everything Lewis had done and promised to continue their support.

But the challenge wasn't over yet.

Lewis had to keep proving he was worth McLaren's support. And this time, he would be racing even further from home!

McLaren and Anthony Hamilton decided that fourteen-year-old Lewis needed to prove how good he was against **the best competition in Europe.** The young drivers from places like France, Italy and Belgium were fast. This was going to be VERY tough!

Lewis Hamilton was quickly becoming a professional racing driver. This was no longer just a boy and his dad going karting. This was the Big Time! Though even out on tour in Europe Lewis still had to do his school homework!

He finished **second** in the most important race of the year, held at the end of the season. McLaren and Ron Dennis remained impressed.

During the season, Lewis had raced against – and beaten – **Nico Rosberg.** Nico would later become Lewis's teammate in F1 and win the World Championship in 2016.

In 2000, Nico's Dad Keke Rosberg put together a team for Nico and Lewis. It was a **karting super-team!** They were ready to take on the best!

Did you know Keke Rosberg, Nico's dad, was F1 World Champion in 1982? The Rosbergs are racing royalty!

Lewis and Nico won a lot of races. At the end of the year, **Lewis was crowned European Formula A Champion** and Nico came second!

Lewis Hamilton was now the **world's No. 1 kart racer.**

Rosberg and Hamilton raced together again in 2001 but, by now, McLaren had thoughts about moving Lewis away from karts and into even faster real racing cars . . .

FORMULA RENAULT AND F3

McLaren chose a **Formula Renault** car for Lewis in 2002. A Formula Renault looked like a miniature Grand Prix car. It had full bodywork with wings at the back and the front. It was much, much faster than even the quickest kart.

The wings on F1 cars are like the opposite of the wings on a plane. They help keep the car down on the ground and stop it going up in the air!

The tyres on a Formula Renault would be 'slicks'; they had no grooves. Grooves are only on a tyre to help get rid of water when it rains. If the track is dry, then the surface of the slick tyre gives lots of grip and helps hold the car to the road. Racing on slicks would be one of the many new things Lewis needed to get used to at this new level of racing.

He was mentored by **John Booth,** who actually gave up life as a butcher to become a racer!

Lewis was fast immediately. He zoomed down the first straight in the Formula Renault, adjusting to the new speed quickly. But on his third lap in the car, he **crashed** and badly damaged the car!

Thankfully, Lewis was unhurt. Crashing is a part of the sport. If you want to get big rewards, you have to take **big risks.** And sometimes that results in a crash. Thankfully, there has been a lot of work to make F1 cars and tracks as safe as possible.

Booth thought Lewis would be slower and more careful when he returned to the track once the car had been repaired. But Booth was shocked when Lewis got back in the cockpit. He accelerated fast and **whizzed** around the circuit on his first go! He'd learned his lesson quickly and made no more mistakes.

It was clear that Lewis had a winning mentality. McLaren and Booth did a deal to have Lewis race in the 2002 British Formula Renault Championship.

Lewis listened and learned during the early races and gradually built up speed. Halfway through 2002, he became **the fastest driver in Formula Renault,** winning pole positions and races.

He would win the British Formula Renault title in 2003 with a commanding season – **10 wins and 11 pole positions in 15 races.** That was very impressive!

Did you know Lewis won his first Formula Renault championship before he actually passed his driving test? As soon as he turned seventeen he officially 'learned' to drive a car. Though it was very different driving on the roads than on a racetrack!

It was quickly time for another step up. Young Lewis was accelerating through his racing career!

Formula Renault cars have 4-cylinder engines. But Formula 3, the next level up, is raced by cars with 6-cylinder engines. Which is a fancy way of saying they feature much faster cars!

Once again, Lewis was going even faster in

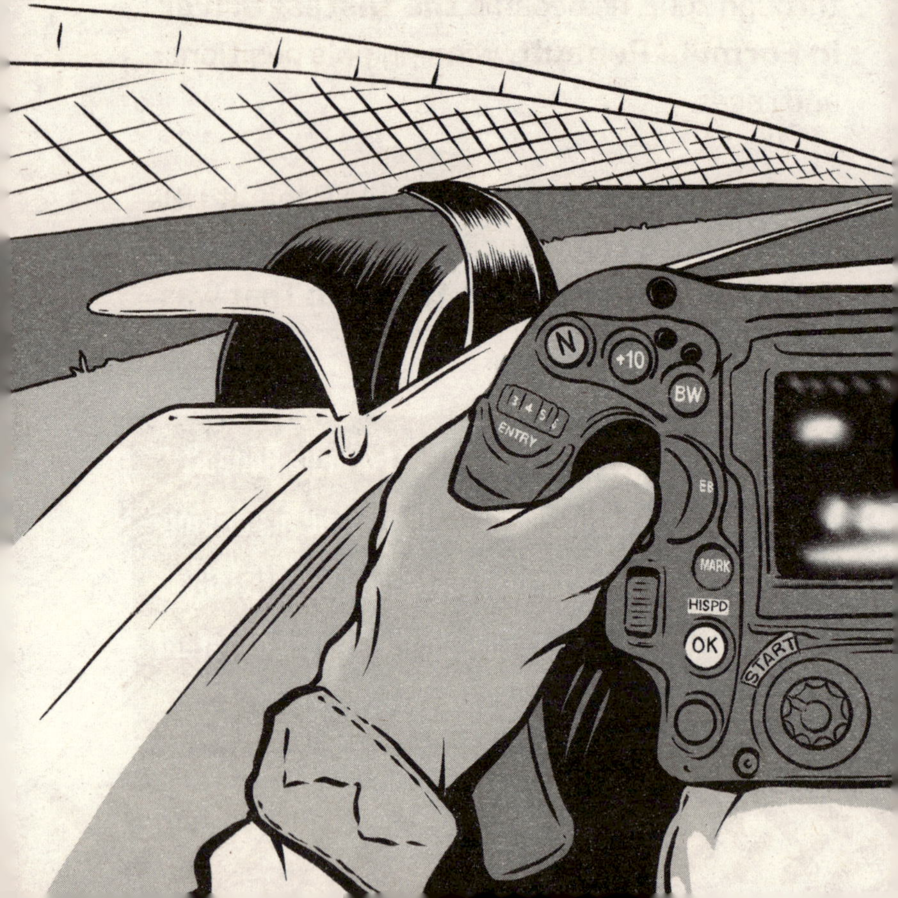

a new formula. In 2005, he moved to the ASM team, the reigning champions in F3, and won the title. **He finished first in 15 of the 20 races!** No one could argue with that!

One more step – and another season like that – and he would be ready for his biggest challenge yet:

Formula 1.

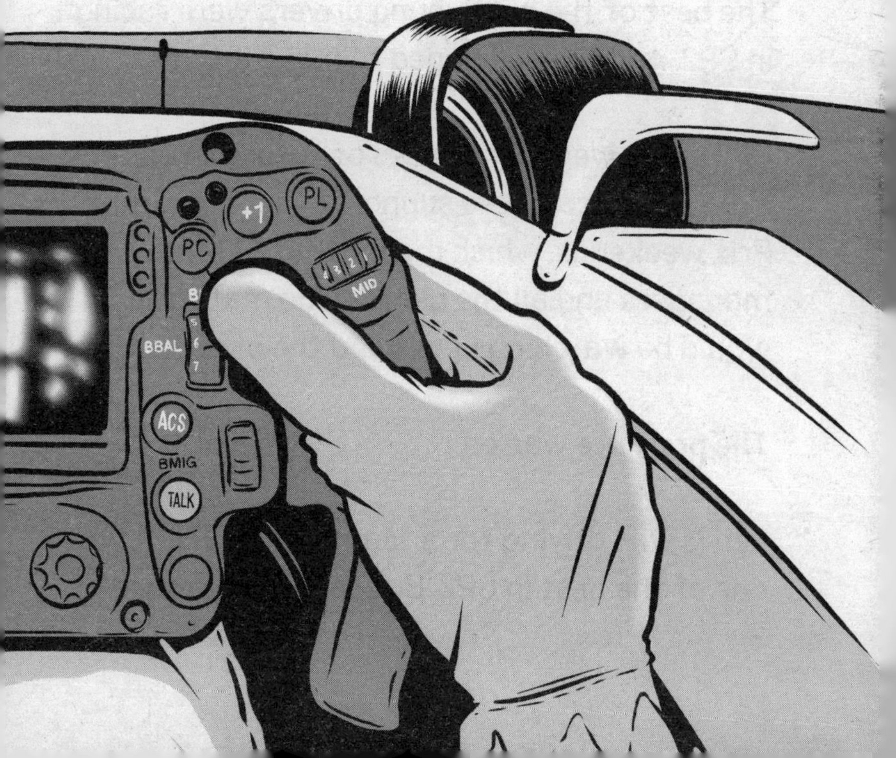

THE FINAL STEP BEFORE F1

GP2 (which is called Formula 2 today) was Lewis's final step to Grand Prix racing. After winning in every championship so far, naturally he was expected to win this new tournament in 2006! But it wouldn't be easy.

The best of the best young drivers were racing in GP2. And they all hoped to make it to F1.

GP2 races were showcases of future talent. Most GP2 races were support events on Grand Prix weekends, which meant that F1 team managers and all the people who mattered would be watching Lewis and the other drivers.

The pressure was on.

Lewis was driving for a team called ART. It was one of the best in GP2. But that didn't mean he would win automatically. He would have to fight every inch of the way. Which he did.

Lewis **dominated** one of the first races of the season, in Germany.

He went on to win the British Grand Prix at Silverstone.

He scored a brilliant **victory** in Monaco in front of the rich and famous.

The great performances kept coming. At another race in Germany, Lewis was brilliant in the rain and managed to finish in second place.

But perhaps his best drive in 2006 was in a race that he actually didn't win.

In Turkey, he spun out early in the race and re-joined in 16th place. It was going to be tough regaining lost ground among such talented drivers. In a brilliant display of fast, powerful driving, he moved to an eventual second place, passing drivers on every side – often when they least expected it! That means **he overtook 14 drivers!** It was truly unbelievable.

After the race, **Michael Schumacher** – the seven-time World Champion and a true Racing Legend – congratulated Lewis on a brilliant drive. Racing drivers do not compliment each other very often. This was big praise!

It was obvious now that the next step for Lewis Hamilton was Formula 1.

He was about to realize his ambition with McLaren and become a Grand Prix driver in 2007.

Everything had been building up to this moment.

Before he could start racing in F1, Lewis was given a test drive in a McLaren Grand Prix car at **Silverstone,** a famous English racetrack.

‘It was an awesome experience,’ said Lewis. ‘I just cannot stop smiling. **I am living my dream.** It’s difficult to describe.’

Despite his winning streak, Lewis Hamilton was still a gamble for McLaren. The world champions liked to use experienced drivers and Lewis was brand new to F1. But it said everything about their faith in Lewis’s speed and potential. Lewis would have a lot of work to do to fit in with the team.

Lewis moved near the McLaren factory and visited it every day. He would talk to the engineers, study computers and understand more about the cars. He learned how the team worked and proved his dedication to being a team player.

Lewis wanted to know about EVERYTHING! He never stopped chasing every detail. **He never stopped learning.** That’s one of the things that makes him a racing legend.

So much of racing is in **attention to detail.**

Grands Prix are won on the finest of margins.

The first Grand Prix in 2007 would be in Melbourne, Australia. That means Lewis made his F1 debut on the other side of the world! Racing had literally taken him very far in life.

Lewis's teammate at McLaren would be **Fernando Alonso.**

Alonso had won many Grands Prix and **two World Championships** and was expected to be quicker than Lewis.

There was much for Lewis to learn now that he had become a Grand Prix driver. He was not expected to win any races at this early stage of his F1 career.

Let's just say, Lewis was about to surprise many people!

LEWIS'S FIRST GRAND PRIX

Ahead of Lewis's first F1 race, there was practice on Friday and again on Saturday morning, before qualifying on Saturday afternoon.

F1 drivers race around the circuit individually during qualifying. The time it takes for them to complete a lap is recorded and their speeds then decide the order that they start the actual race. The faster you are in qualifying, the closer to the front of the race you start the next day.

It was raining at the start of Friday's practice. Lewis had never driven an F1 car in wet conditions before. Because the track was wet, the McLaren would have less grip on the road. The powerful engine would make the car slide more if Lewis pushed the throttle too hard.

This was big pressure, with the world watching to see how he got on. Lewis did not put a foot wrong.

He was even more impressive on Saturday afternoon, **qualifying fourth for his first Grand Prix.** Usually, you'd expect a new driver to be further down the grid as he got used to

F1 and the more powerful car.

Lewis was only a little slower than Alonso, who got second place. People began to take notice. Already, people were remembering Hamilton's name.

But qualifying was nothing compared to racing in the actual Grand Prix.

58 laps.

307 km (191 miles).

21 world class drivers.

It was going to be a very different challenge!

Everyone thought Lewis would be **cautious** – particularly at the start. The last thing he would want on his first race would be to **crash.** If he did, people would immediately say that he was not ready for F1. They would blame McLaren for bringing him into F1 much too soon. There was **a lot of pressure** on him.

But when the race began Lewis, starting in fourth position, sped fast into the first corner, overtaking his teammate Alonso – coming out of the corner in third place right at the start of the race!

Fernando was not expecting this and neither was anyone else . . .

This was not Lewis being crazy or overexcited. It was a sign of how good he was at **seeing opportunities to overtake.** It showed how quickly he could make **important decisions and judgements.** From his very first turn on an F1 racetrack, it was clear that there was a new champion on the cards.

The start and first corner are the most dramatic moments of any Grand Prix. Lewis had been **inch-perfect** during this high-pressure moment.

He stayed calm for the next hour and a half despite reaching 300 kmh (190 mph) in places on the Melbourne racetrack! Can you imagine going that fast?

For the first part of the race, he had Alonso – a **double world champion** – right behind him. Alonso was waiting for a single mistake by Lewis.

If Lewis slipped up once, Alonso would pounce and overtake him.

But he didn't make a single mistake.

It was only due to McLaren's team that Alonso could overtake Lewis during pit stops. It was part of their game plan. Lewis didn't mind this. He was focussed on learning about the demands of F1.

The Grand Prix was longer and tougher than any race he had ever done before. The race was three or four times longer than any of the kart races he'd done!

The race was won by the Ferrari driver, **Kimi Räikkönen.**

Did you know Kimi Räikkönen had only competed in 23 races – ever! – when he made his F1 debut in 2001. He went on to win 21 Grands Prix and the championship in 2007.

Alonso finished second.

Lewis came home third.

That meant he **finished on the podium** for his very first Grand Prix! That was super rare for a brand-new F1 driver.

After Lewis had received his trophy and **huge cheers** from the crowd, his father was waiting for him. It was a special moment for them both.

It was 14 years since Anthony had guided Lewis through his first kart race at the age of eight. They had come a long way since then. Lewis focussing on becoming a better, faster driver.

Anthony working hard to find the money and support for his son.

And here he was on a Grand Prix podium!

All that hard work had paid off.

Now that he had come third, the next question on everybody's minds was: could Lewis Hamilton win a Grand Prix?

After everything they had seen in Australia, people were beginning to believe that he could! Within one race, he'd made a name for himself.

There would be 16 more Grands Prix in 2007. That was 16 more chances to move his way up to the top of the podium.

Could he get there in his first ever F1 season?

Lewis continued his incredible F1 debut by **finishing SECOND at the next two races** in **Malaysia** and **Bahrain.**

He was **joint leader of the World Championship** leader boards with Alonso and Räikkönen!

The race in Malaysia had been very tough. It was run in **hot and humid** conditions. Lewis had never raced in these conditions before – certainly not for a race lasting 90 minutes! That's as long as a football game!

Did you know that each driver uses a tube in the front of his crash helmet to suck liquid from a bottle behind his seat?

Drivers get **very hot** in an F1 race. No air gets into the very tight cockpit of an F1 car which makes it so hot that F1 drivers will sweat **two litres** during a Grand Prix. That's *insane*!

All that sweat means that drivers need to stay hydrated! This is very important – otherwise the driver will lose concentration. And losing concentration when you're racing at 300 kmh (186 mph) could lead to **disaster.**

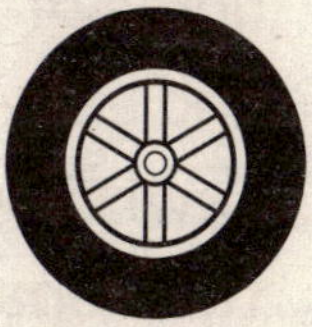

In Malaysia, Lewis finished his drink too early on in the race. He had to complete the final half hour without liquid. It was becoming **hotter** and **hotter** in the cockpit. And he was under **intense pressure** from Räikkönen, who was right behind him. Lewis somehow managed to hold on to second place, despite the crazy heat. It was yet another amazing performance!

The second-place finishes continued for Lewis in **Bahrain** and then **Spain.** He looked more confident than ever! He was getting very comfortable up on the podium. But he wouldn't stop striving until he was the very best.

The next Grand Prix after Spain took place in the streets of **Monaco.**

Monaco is the biggest test for any Grand Prix driver. In many ways the city is the glamorous home of F1, with its big yachts in the harbour and expensive houses and hotels. It's a circuit Lewis loved. He had won races in F2 and F3 on the Monaco track. Why not F1?

The McLarens were the fastest cars at Monaco all weekend during practice and qualifying. Alonso took pole position, with Hamilton in second place. Lewis felt certain pole position would have been his had he not been caught behind a slower car during qualifying.

Because of the narrow street circuit, overtaking is very difficult at Monaco. If a driver starts from pole and doesn't make any mistakes, in theory he should win. Of course, overtaking was a key part of Hamilton's game plan. But he had to wait for Alonso to make a mistake, which he didn't. In the race, Alonso finished first and Lewis held on to second place.

Second at the Monaco Grand Prix in your first

F1 season is a fantastic achievement. But Lewis was not happy. He felt he could have won had he been able to start from pole position and not been held up during qualifying.

'Never mind,' said Lewis. 'I'll win next time.'

The next race was in Canada.

And now Lewis had something to prove.

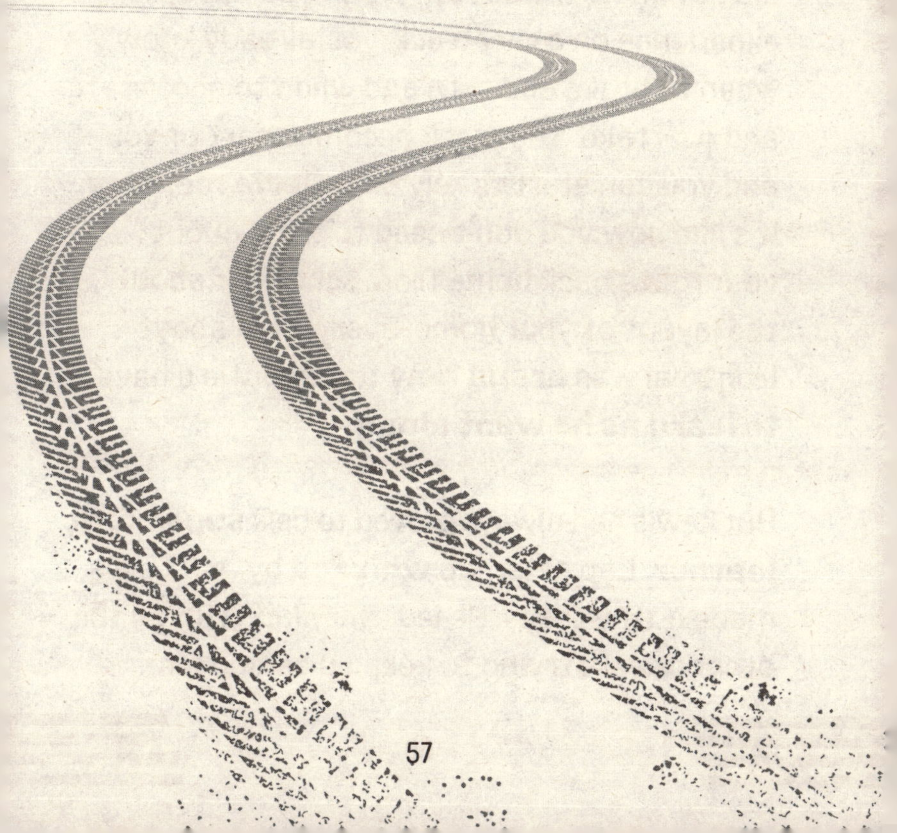

LEWIS'S FIRST F1 WIN

The Canadian Grand Prix is held in **Montreal.** The track is located on an island in the middle of the St Lawrence river.

Lewis had never raced in Montreal before. Unlike Alonso and most of his rivals, Lewis did not know the circuit. When you have experience on a racetrack, you already know when to brake and turn and when to accelerate and overtake. The track becomes part of you, and you can start to rely on **muscle memory.** It's like how you don't need to think about your route back home from school, or about the layout of your home. Everything about Montreal was **brand new** to Lewis. He'd have to **learn as he went along.**

But Lewis had always proved to be a **super-fast learner.** Lap after lap **whizzed** by and Lewis made no mistakes. He led every lap, with all the other drivers trying to keep up behind him.

But it wasn't an easy race.

There was a problem on the track.

A big one.

Robert Kubica was involved in a crash in his BMW.

This meant a **Safety Car** came onto the track to **slow down the race.** This allowed the track marshals to attend to the incident.

Did you know that you aren't allowed to overtake while the Safety Car is on the track?

Lewis knew Kubica very well. He had raced against the Polish driver when they were in karting. He liked Robert a lot.

It took a while to remove Kubica from the wreckage. Lewis could see this each time **the field** – the stream of F1 cars going slowly behind the Safety Car – passed the scene of the accident.

Lewis was very happy to hear that Robert had not been badly hurt. It was a minor miracle.

Now Lewis had to make sure he remained focussed for the moment when the Safety Car pulled off the circuit and the race got going again.

All the other drivers were close behind him now.

Despite the pressure of his first win getting close, Lewis remained **incredibly calm.**

And **incredibly fast.**

As soon as the Safety Car period was over he **zoomed** along the track, and managed to hold on to the lead of the race!

He was thrilled when he saw **the chequered flag being waved for him.**

Lewis Hamilton: Grand Prix Winner!

Lewis dedicated the win to his dad and thanked him for all his support. It was a huge moment for father and son after all they had been through together.

To make it even better, Lewis Hamilton was now **leading the World Championship.** He was ahead of some of the biggest Racing Legends in the world, after just six F1 races!

He would go on to end the season second in the World Championship, just one point behind Kimi Räikkönen. To end the year **on the podium** was simply unbelievable.

THE SILVER ARROWS

In his first F1 season in 2007, Lewis raced a McLaren car **powered by a Mercedes engine.**

In 2013, Lewis would move to the Mercedes team and break records for winning races and championships.

Mercedes has a **legendary history** in motor racing. The German team has been racing for a VERY long time.

More than 100 years ago, Mercedes won the French Grand Prix. It was the first of many wins for Mercedes.

Did you know that the Mercedes name came from a person called Mercédès Jellinek? She was the daughter of Emil Jellinek, the man who designed the car.

Imagine having a car named after you! If you designed a brand-new car, what would you call it?

The Mercedes name became one of the greatest in motor racing.

At first, Mercedes cars were white, and then silver. They were known as the **Silver Arrows** because they were so so fast.

Each time new rules were made for Grand Prix cars, Mercedes would make better, faster cars than anyone else.

They did this 90 years ago.

They did it again in the 1950s.

Each time **the Silver Arrows were unbeatable.**

Mercedes left the world of motor racing for a while. They came back in the 1990s, making engines for F1 teams including McLaren.

But in 2010, Mercedes formed their own team once more. They won the Chinese Grand Prix in 2012. The car, driven by **Nico Rosberg,** gave Mercedes their **first win in 57 years!**

Lewis Hamilton joined the historic Mercedes team in 2013. In 2014, they began a fantastic winning streak together. **Lewis became World Champion in 2014 and 2015.**

Nico Rosberg – who Lewis had raced against in karting – won the championship for Mercedes in 2016. He was Lewis's teammate – but the two of them fought hard, competing to win, right up to the last race of the season.

Lewis Hamilton won the championship again in:

2017 . . .

2018 . . .

2019 . . .

. . . and 2020.

What a streak!

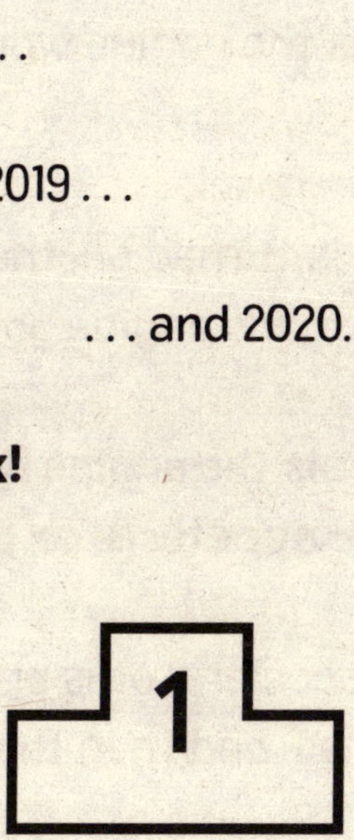

UNDER THE HOOD!

Think of a car like a body.

The **engine is the heart of the car.**

And the **driver is the brain.**

The driver makes the engine work. Then the car can move.

Once the engine is turned on, the driver controls how fast the engine goes.

The driver controls the engine by pressing their right foot on the **accelerator pedal.**

The harder the accelerator is pressed, the faster the engine – and then the car – will go.

This happens in cars you see on the roads near you.

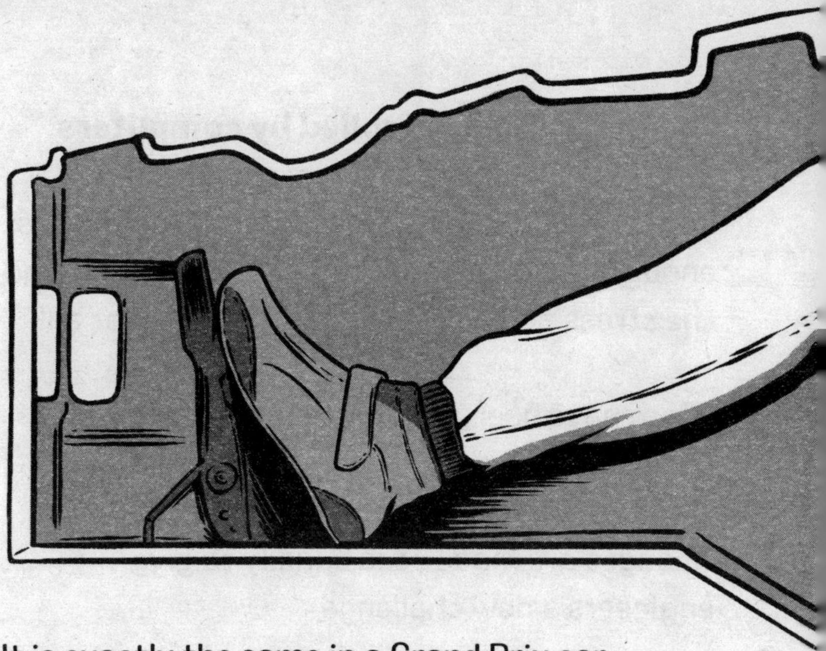

It is exactly the same in a Grand Prix car. Lewis Hamilton pushes his right foot on the accelerator to make his F1 car go faster.

The difference is **the engine in Lewis's Grand Prix car is VERY powerful.** It makes the Mercedes reach speeds of up to 320 kmh (199 mph).

Engines are specially made for Grand Prix racing cars. They need to work very hard to allow the driver to go quickly and win races.

Engines in F1 cars used to be very simple.

Today, they are **controlled by computers.** If an F1 engine from 50 years ago was put in Lewis Hamilton's Mercedes, it would not be fast enough. It would break because of the heat and the stress and he wouldn't get very far at all!

There have been different types of engines allowed in F1 during the past 100 years.

Changes are made occasionally to give engineers a new challenge.

Much of the engine technology today is all about **electric engines.** These are run on batteries. They do not burn fuel and are **better for the environment.**

Did you know F1 cars can use 110 kilograms of fuel per race? As the fuel gets used up, the cars get lighter, which means their fastest laps are normally towards the end of the race.

The engines used in F1 at the moment are called **Hybrid.** They are a combination of engines powered by petrol and electricity.

With each change, the engines get better and better. They become **faster, more powerful and more reliable.** That's thanks to the work of **engineers.** In many ways, engineers are just as important to a team's success as the drivers themselves!

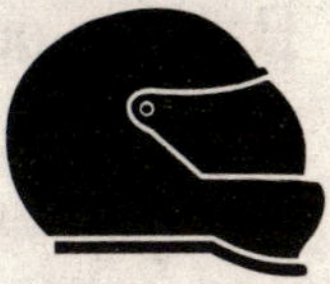

Improved F1 engines have also led to better engines in cars you see in your streets. Everybody wins!

HOW AN ENGINE WORKS

Cars have changed a lot in the past 100 years. But the purpose of the engine has remained the same. It provides the power to make the car go.

How exactly does this work?

Fuel is added to a **chamber** inside the engine. This chamber is known as the **cylinder.**

Inside the cylinder is a **piston,** which goes up and down.

When the piston reaches the top of the cylinder, it crushes a mix of fuel and **air** which has been allowed into the cylinder.

A spark causes an **explosion** as it ignites the **compressed mix of fuel and air** in

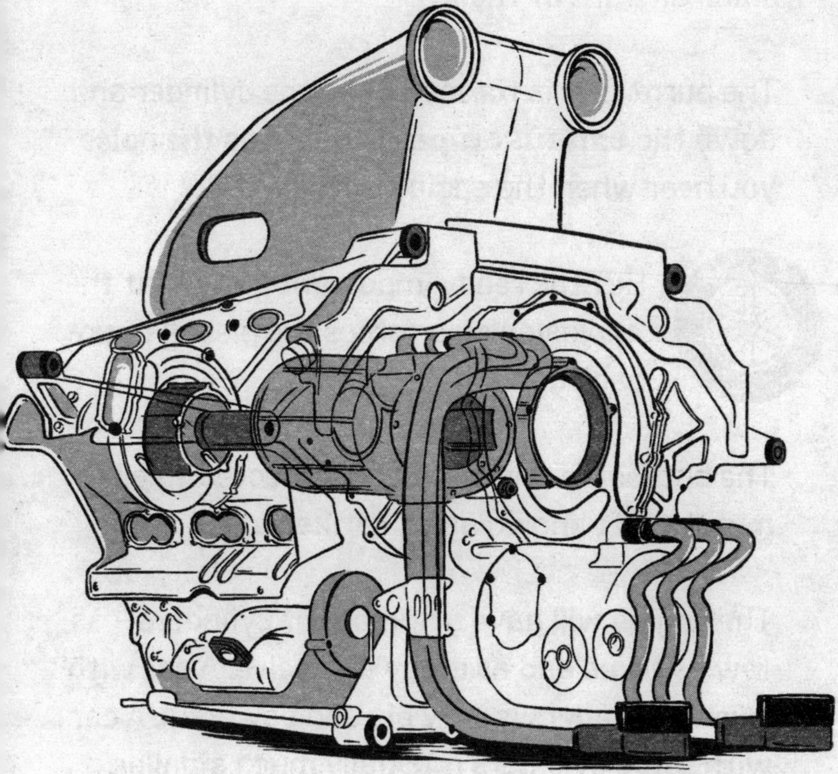

the cylinder. But this is not as dangerous as it sounds! The explosion is safely contained inside the cylinder in what is called the **combustion chamber.** It involves a very small amount of fuel.

The burnt fuel is forced out of the cylinder and down the **exhaust pipe.** This makes the noise you hear when the engine is running.

But the really important bit is that the explosion also forces the piston to go back down the cylinder.

The bottom of the piston is connected to a big metal shaft known as a **crankshaft.**

The engine will have a number of cylinders – as few as three and as many as twelve. A car with twelve cylinders is very big and powerful. A car with three cylinders is usually much smaller, and slower.

The crankshaft runs under the engine and connects all of the pistons at the bottom of each cylinder. The explosion in each cylinder – the explosions happen one after the other, not all at the same time! – moves the pistons, which then turn the crankshaft.

This begins the movement which eventually turns the car's wheels and makes it move.

These explosions cause heat in the cylinders. That's why **cooling** is important to prevent the engine getting too hot. Cooling is done by **water** circulating around the engine.

The hot water then passes through **radiators,** which are cooled by **air** being forced through them as the car travels at speed.

This is the same, whether it is on a road car or on Lewis Hamilton's F1 car. Of course, because Lewis's car goes much faster, the engine works much harder and needs more cooling.

The power of an engine is measured by what is called **horsepower.**

The bigger the engine – or the more cylinders it has – the more powerful it will be and the more horsepower it will have.

The power of a horse has nothing to do with car engines. Horsepower is an old-fashioned term, from back when people used horses, not cars to get around!

Hundreds of years ago, horsepower referred to the power of a horse being able to pull a rope and raise a certain weight from the ground via a pulley. But the phrase 'horsepower' continues to be used when talking about the power of engines.

When Lewis was racing karts, the tiny engine in his **Cadet kart** developed between 5 and 10 horsepower (known as **10 bhp**).

A **Mini Cooper** develops about **100 bhp.**

Lewis Hamilton's **F1 Mercedes** engine produces more than **1000 bhp!**

THE SILVER WAR

Lewis Hamilton and Nico Rosberg have been **great rivals** throughout their racing careers.

They come from very different backgrounds.

Nico was born in West Germany, just six months after Lewis in 1985. Nico's father, Keke, had been the **1982 F1 World Champion.** Keke was from Finland. Nico's mother is German and Nico can speak five languages: English, German, Finnish, French and Italian.

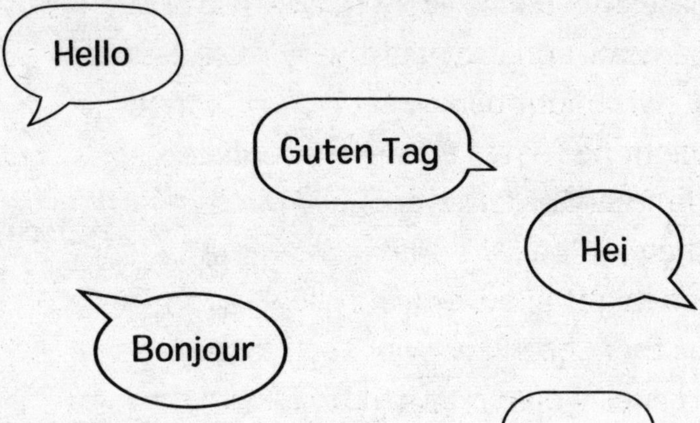

Like Lewis, Nico began racing with karting and won lots of championships. Along the way, he raced against Lewis. They became teammates as early as 2000.

They spent a lot of time together. They were good friends but were competitive in everything they did. And I mean everything! They would even race to see who could finish their pizza first!

The rivalry became very serious in 2016. Nico and Lewis were driving together at Mercedes.

Mercedes had two top drivers knowing that the fastest would be likely to win. The driver that came out on top might vary from race to race. Lewis might be quicker in, say, Monaco. Nico might be faster at the next race in Canada. Team orders were used by the team when having their drivers race each other for the lead might allow a rival following closely to pass them both and win! Team orders by Mercedes would tell their drivers to hold position, particularly towards the end of a race. That way the team would win, even if Lewis had to settle for second.

But during the 2016 season, **there were no team orders.**

Whoever was fastest would win.

Lewis had beaten Nico to the championship in 2014 and 2015. Nico was determined to put that right in 2016. He won the first four races. The battle was on!

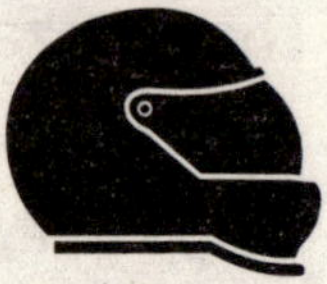

But this rivalry wasn't just fierce, it was dangerous. The two Mercedes drivers actually **collided** while fighting for the lead of the Spanish Grand Prix. There was nothing to choose between them.

Going into the final round of the 2016 championship, Rosberg was leading Hamilton by 12 points on the championship table. Lewis led the race but Nico only needed to finish third to become champion. Nico's position came under attack – but he managed to hold on to second place and **win the championship** by five points!

Then, a day later, **Nico retired from Grand Prix racing.** He had achieved his goal. He had beaten Lewis in their most important battle.

But you can decide for yourself who the better driver is . . . !

HAMILTON

Born	7.1.85
First Grand Prix	2007 Australia
First World Championship points	2007 Australia
First F1 podium	2007 Australia
First Pole Position	2007 Canada
Pole Positions	104
First Fastest Lap	2007 Malaysia
Fastest Laps	65
Laps in the lead	5,570+
First F1 win	2007 Canada
Most F1 wins in a season	11 (2014, 2018, 2019, 2020)
F1 wins	103
F1 Podiums	195
F1 World Championships	7
Championship points	4550+
Grands Prix raced	325+

***Vs* ROSBERG**

27.6.85
2006 Bahrain
2006 Bahrain
2008 Australia
2012 China
30
2006 Bahrain
20
1525
2012 China
9 (2016)
23
57
1
1594.5
206

A QUICK PIT STOP

Pit stops were necessary right from the start of Grand Prix racing more than 100 years ago.

The races were **loooong** and drivers needed to stop for more fuel and new tyres to be able to keep going. They could be driving for three or four hours!

The pit stops could take several minutes back then. There would only be one or two **mechanics** and they would have to change one wheel at a time. Driving that fast for that long would wear the tyres out. It's kind of like a long-distance runner wearing through their trainers, and needing to stop for new shoes!

When Grand Prix distances were cut to 300 km (190 miles), it became possible for a driver to go the whole race without stopping.

But it was actually faster if a driver could stop

for fresh tyres – provided the pit stop did not take too long.

This led to carefully rehearsed pit stops in which a driver can have his wheels changed in **less than two seconds.** That's less time than it's taken you to read this sentence! Blink – and you'll miss it!

Did you know, there can be as many as twenty-three pit crew involved each time a car makes a pit stop? That means there could be almost 230 pit crew in total for each race!

As soon as the car stops, the front and rear are raised instantly by mechanics with **jacks.**

Three mechanics work on each wheel.

One loosens the **wheel nut . . .**

A second removes the old tyre . . .

And a third puts the new tyre in place ready for one of the others to tighten the nut.

A mechanic standing on each side of the car will keep it steady while the tyre changing takes place.

The speed and violence of the **wheel guns** will shake the car.

The **wheel guns** are so fast and powerful that they can break a mechanic's wrist if not held properly.

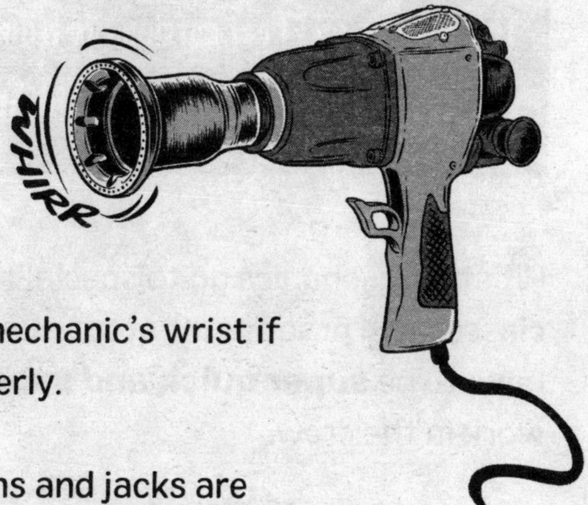

The wheel guns and jacks are connected electronically. As soon as the wheel changes are finished, a green light is triggered and the driver accelerates away with **minimum time loss.**

A **manager** watches the pit stop and can halt the process if something goes wrong. Or, if the electronic system fails, they can wave the car away.

It is also possible – if necessary – to change the car's **nose and front wings.** This can be done in seconds.

The nose on an F1 car carries the front wings, which help give more grip to the front wheels.

Pit stop mechanics go to special fitness classes and practise pit stops every day! You have to be **super quick and super strong** to work in the crew.

Fast pit stops are vital to winning a race. The racing is so close that the smallest mistake during a pit stop could cost the team a win.

It is MASSIVE pressure. But it involves the whole team. Winning a Grand Prix is not just about the driver! **It's a team effort.** From the engineers, to the pit stop mechanics, to the driver themselves.

Each F1 team is made up of between 500 and 1,000 people. They will design, build and make the two cars ready to race in each Grand Prix. It's not just the driver who wins the race!

SILVERSTONE

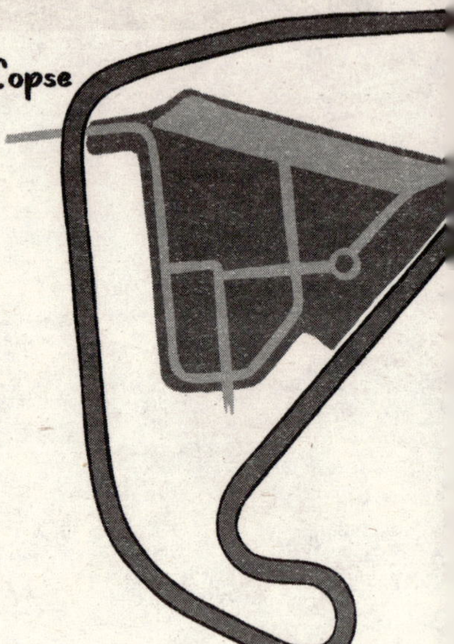

Silverstone is one of the most famous racetracks in the world.

Silverstone staged **the very first round of the F1 World Championship in 1950.**

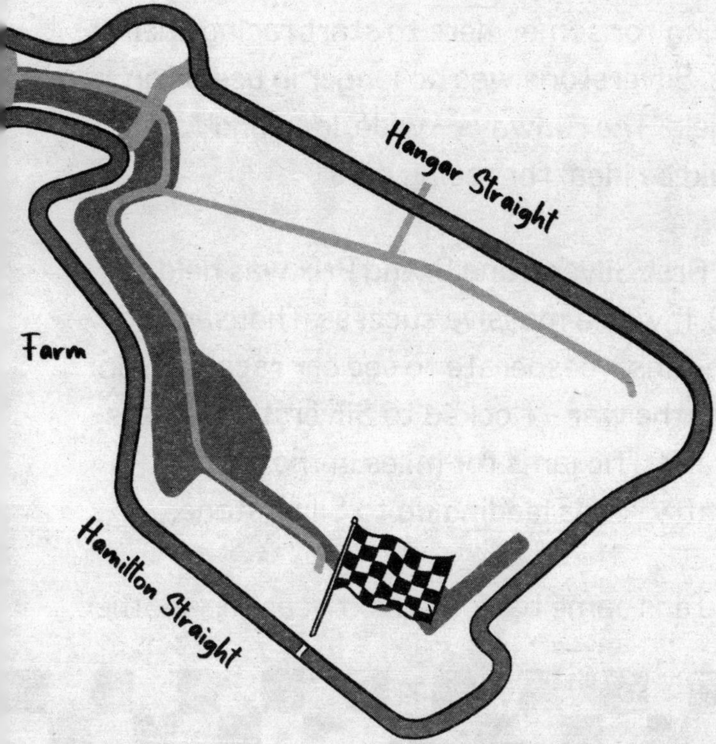

The flat, very fast track is in a central position, right in the middle of England. Silverstone has long straights and fast corners. Some tracks, like Monaco, are the opposite with lots of tight corners and very few straights. Which means F1 cars can reach **very high speeds** at Silverstone for long periods of time.

It was originally an airfield, built for use in the **Second World War** between 1939 and 1945.

When the war ended, motor-sport fans were looking for somewhere to start racing their cars. Silverstone was no longer in use as an airfield. The runways – wide, long and fast – would be ideal for racing cars!

The first Silverstone Grand Prix was held in 1948. It was a massive success. Thousands of race fans – desperate to see car racing again after the war – flocked to Silverstone. There were traffic jams for miles in the narrow country roads leading up to Silverstone.

The fans came back the next year for another

Grand Prix in 1949. The race attracted star drivers and teams from Italy, France and other European countries.

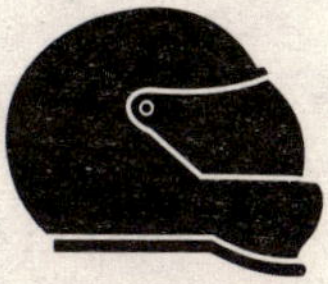

Silverstone became really famous in 1950. The people in charge of world motor racing wanted to start the World Championship we have today. They chose Silverstone to host the very first World Championship Grand Prix in 1950.

Did you know, there have been more than 50 Grands Prix at Silverstone? It has always been one of the fastest circuits on the F1 calendar.

The track has been improved, made safer and changed a lot. The runways were used for the first few years. Then the track was made up by a road around the edge of the airfield.

The British Grand Prix at Silverstone is one of the most popular on the F1 calendar. **480,000** people came through the gates during the 2023 British GP weekend.

A HISTORIC RACE

The first World Championship race at Silverstone was a HUGE occasion. It was the very first round of the F1 World Championship. There have been more than 1,000 Grands Prix since then all around the world.

The race was actually known as 'The Grand Prix of Europe'. This was in honour of the significance of the race. The Grand Prix in May 1950 was attended by **King George VI and Queen Elizabeth.**

Did you know, this was the first motor race ever attended by a British King and Queen? It was that important! The race would be known in the newspapers as 'Royal Silverstone'.

The entry included red **Maseratis** and **Alfa Romeos** from Italy, and blue **Talbot-Lagos** from France. British drivers raced green British cars such as the **ERA** (English Racing Automobiles). Back then F1 cars were shaped very differently, and could achieve speeds of **257 kmh (160 mph).**

Alfa Romeo make road cars in Italy. They stopped F1 racing in the 1950s and returned for a while in the 1970s. The Alfa Romeo name is still in F1 today. They took over the Sauber F1 team in 2019.

More than **100,000** spectators stood in the fields surrounding the 2.8-mile long track. There were very few grandstands and poor facilities. But no one cared! This was a big motor race and a lot of fun!

The Grand Prix took more than two hours. The cars made many pit stops for fuel and tyres. Most pit stops would last at least a couple of minutes back then. Lewis Hamilton and Mercedes will only take two seconds for a pit stop today!

The race was won by **Giuseppe Farina.** Farina was a talented man from Italy. As well as being an F1 driver, he was also a lawyer and an officer in the Italian army.

Farina was driving an Alfa Romeo and would become the **first ever World Champion** in 1950.

SUPERSHELL
22

HAMILTON'S GREAT BRITISH GRAND PRIX

The 2008 British Grand Prix at Silverstone was one of **Lewis Hamilton's GREATEST races.**

Lewis had narrowly lost the championship in 2007. He came to Silverstone as favourite to win his home race.

Things did not get off to a good start when he only qualified in fourth place. Lewis's McLaren teammate, **Heikki Kovalainen,** was starting in pole position.

Lewis made a brilliant start and quickly moved into second place behind Kovalainen. The track was wet and slippery – the conditions were treacherous.

Several drivers had incidents or **spun off.** But not

Lewis. By lap 5, he had overtaken his teammate and was in the lead. And he was pulling away. There was nothing Kovalainen could do about it.

In 111 F1 starts, Heikki Kovalainen only won one race.

Halfway through the race, Hamilton was challenged by the Ferrari of **Kimi Räikkönen,** the reigning World Champion.

Then the rain got worse.

Hamilton extended his lead as Räikkönen dropped back, unable to keep up with the flying McLaren.

No one could touch Hamilton. Showing incredible skill in the slippery conditions, Lewis was **in a class of his own.** Cars were spinning into the gravel and slipping on the tarmac.

Kimi Räikkönen, aka 'The Iceman', is the most successful Finnish F1 driver in history, having won twenty-one Grands Prix.

But nothing could stop the leading McLaren. Hamilton just went faster and faster.

He won by more than a minute. **That's a MASSIVE margin.** It was a brilliant demonstration of Lewis's **skill** and **control.**

It was his seventh F1 win. And one of his greatest.

Lewis said it was one of his **proudest moments** as he stood on the top step of the podium and the British National Anthem rang out across Silverstone. The Racing Legend had won in style on his home turf.

A LEGEND AMONG LEGENDS

Felipe MASSA:

(Hamilton's championship rival in 2008):

'What he does with the car is just different. It is similar to Ayrton Senna. There is something that brings a **perfection** that is really hard to achieve. Yet he is able to do it.'

Charles LECLERC:

'Lewis is **very smart.** The way he positions the car around a bend. He is less aggressive but thinks more about how to do it. If he doesn't overtake you at one point it's because he's thinking of another, simpler way in which to attack. He has always been **respectful** to me – and anyone he meets. That should be the standard.'

Lando NORRIS:

'When I was growing up, you always used to hear the stories about Ayrton Senna or Michael Schumacher and how great they were. Now it's Lewis Hamilton. **He's one of the greatest, ever.'**

George RUSSELL:

'I've nothing but admiration for Lewis. I feel incredibly fortunate to be with a team such as Mercedes and to have Lewis as a teammate. He has **pushed me to new levels.** He's really made me raise my game as a driver.'

Sergio PEREZ:

'Racing against Lewis, I've been fortunate enough to see how good he is. The way he pushes you. The way he can go fast and save his tyres. He's obviously a **very, very intelligent** guy.'

Max VERSTAPPEN:

'You have to acknowledge that the way Lewis has consistently beaten his teammate, he's done an **amazing job.'**

Damon HILL:

(1996 F1 World Champion):

'Lewis is **the greatest racer we've ever produced.** Year-in, year-out, he's delivered in all situations. He is properly formidable as a competitor.'

HAMILTON'S WINNING HISTORY

- First win – Canada, 2007
- Won 4 times in his first season
- Won 5 times in 2008, the year of his first championship
- Won races in every season, from 2007–2021
- Won from pole 61 times
- 50th win – America, 2016

- 91st win (equalling Michael Schumacher's record) – Eifel GP in Germany, 2020
- 100th win – Russia, 2021
- Won 8 times at Silverstone and the Hungaroring
- Won 11 times in 2014, 2018, 2019 and 2020

HAMILTON'S HEROES

The sportsperson who inspires Lewis most is **Muhammad Ali.**

Muhammad Ali was a professional boxer in the 1960s and 1970s. The American is regarded as one of the **greatest heavyweight boxers of all time.**

Lewis never met Ali but has read all about him and watched films of his fights – some of which are remembered as the most **brave** and **skilful** ever seen.

Several of Ali's fights have gone down as the greatest in the history of boxing. Many of the fights drew record TV and film audiences of several million.

Ali is remembered for the way he spoke openly about his faith and his love of poetry. He was also an influential figure in the world of hip hop music.

'Muhammad Ali was my favourite sportsperson – ever,' says Lewis. 'I go onto the internet and watch clips of him. I love watching those kind of old-school things when you try to understand what was going on back then. How cool was Ali! I would love to be like that. He was inspirational. I never met him but would love to have done.

'The style that Ali had, and the way he was such a hero, matters to me so much.'

LEWIS'S CHARITY WORK

Lewis Hamilton's status as a legend goes beyond the racing track. He's not just an inspiration when he's driving a car, he also drives for **social change.**

Lewis Hamilton founded **Mission 44** in 2021. It's a charitable foundation to help young people.

Mission 44 aims to provide a **fairer, more inclusive future** in which every young person can thrive, regardless of their background or learning difficulties.

Lewis is a prominent advocate for increasing diversity in motor-sport. Mission 44 works with the Mercedes F1 team in a joint charitable foundation called **Ignite** by offering **educational opportunities and financial support** to budding young drivers.

He also established **The Hamilton Commission.** The commission works with the Royal Academy of Engineering to find ways in which motor-sport can engage with more young Black people.

Lewis also works with **UNICEF,** the United Nations Children's Fund. After the 2012 Malaysian Grand Prix, he flew to the Philippines and visited children on the streets of Manila. It was part of Lewis's mission to help children not being fed properly in poor countries. Lewis raised nearly £5m to help the starving children in the Philippines.

Lewis makes regular visits to hospitals for sick children and is a Global Ambassador for **Save The Children,** supporting and promoting its educational aims.

He regularly attends charitable functions and formed a foundation to help provide grants and donations for many charitable causes.

Giving back to the community is an important part of Lewis's success. It's not just about making it yourself. It's about bringing others up with you.

F1 FITNESS

Believe it or not an F1 driver has to be **one of the fittest athletes in sport.** It's not just sitting down and steering!

A driver undergoes **HUGE** forces on his body when racing an F1 car.

The acceleration is massive. So are the forces on the car when braking for a corner.

When cornering, the sideways forces on a driver's body cause drivers to experience **five times their weight** pressing in on them. This happens every few seconds, particularly on fast circuits.

Drivers need to have very **strong necks** and **immense core strength** in their bodies as they're constantly being pulled and pushed in different directions, very quickly.

They must have **strong heart muscles** to withstand a high heart rate throughout races lasting for an hour and a half.

Each driver will have their own fitness programme and personal trainer.

They will do **pull-ups, press-ups** and **bench press** lifts to develop their arms and shoulders.

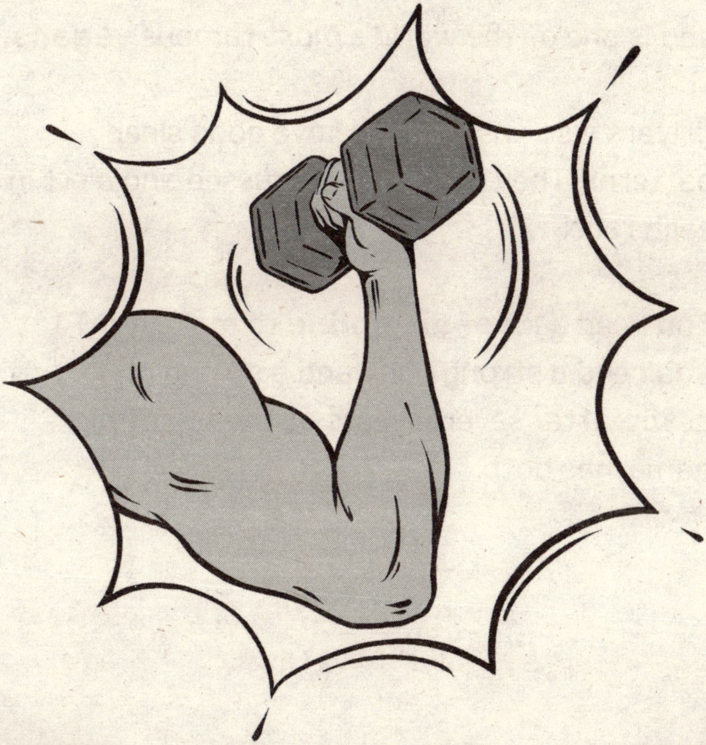

There will also be exercises to strengthen leg muscles. Drivers need to deliver an incredible force on the brake pedal several times every lap.

Drivers will do lots of **running** and **cycling** when not in the gym.

Drivers watch what they eat very carefully. Lewis switched to a **plant-based diet** in 2018 and is one of the world's most famous **vegans.**

Drivers also ensure they have good sleep patterns. They have to be focussed and alert in each race.

You need a lot of **discipline** to make it in F1. You need a strong body and a strong mind. Lewis, after several years at the top of his game, has both.

HAMILTON'S HEROES

Ayrton Senna, one of Lewis Hamilton's heroes, was F1 **World Champion three times.**

He drove most of his F1 races with McLaren, the same team Lewis raced for when he made his F1 debut and won his first championship.

Senna came from Brazil and raced in Europe, winning championships in karting and junior racing.

He was very, very fast and spectacular, with many fans around the world.

There were races when Senna was so fast, no other driver could get close to beating him.

Senna wore a distinctive yellow crash helmet. Lewis had similar colours on his helmet when he started in F1.

Senna was involved in big battles with **Alain Prost** when they were McLaren teammates in 1989, and when Prost moved to Ferrari in 1990.

Senna won **forty-one Grands Prix** in total, making him a historic racing legend. He was Lewis Hamilton's idol.

Did you know French racing legend Alain Prost would have been a footballer if he hadn't tried driving a kart and loved it? He was F1 world champion in 1985, 1986, 1989 and 1993.

Lewis was deeply shocked when Senna was killed during the 1994 San Marino Grand Prix at Imola in Italy.

Lewis was just nine years old when he was watching that race. It was his first lesson in how dangerous motor racing can be, no matter how skilful and careful you are as a driver.

The stakes couldn't be higher. F1 isn't just win or lose. Sometimes it's life and death.

HOW MUCH DOES AN F1 CAR COST?

You can't buy an F1 car in a car showroom, so there's no price tag. It's impossible to say accurately just how much one car costs to make.

Teams are limited by the regulations to spending around **£100 million** in a year. This includes **designing** and **building** the cars.

The **engine** is the most expensive part. These can cost **£12 million each.**

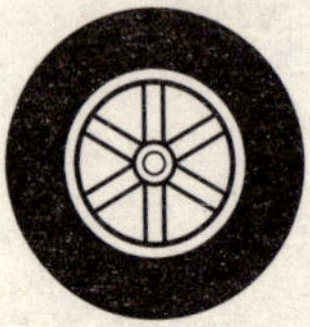

The **chassis** – where the driver sits – is made of very strong but light material. One chassis can cost £500,000.

The **gearbox** is very complex and powered by electronics. A team can spend £250,000 just on the gearbox alone.

The **steering wheel** has more than **twenty buttons, paddles and settings** to control many parts of the car's performance. It's like the world's most complicated game controller! Each steering wheel costs £40,000.

An F1 car's **nose and front wing** are very complex and can cost £100,000 each.

The **fuel tank,** which must be almost **indestructible** to prevent spillage and a fire during an accident, will cost at least £20,000.

A set of four **tyres** costs more than £2,000. A driver can use as many **as thirteen sets** during a Grand Prix weekend. That's going to cost the team at least £26,000 for each driver at every race. There are more than 20 races each season. That's at least £520,000 on tyres each year!

It's safe to say, F1 is a BIG money sport.

Can you add up all those prices and estimate the total cost for one F1 car?

A VERY WET GRAND PRIX

When the weather changes during a Grand Prix, the driver must be using the best tyres for the conditions.

If the track is wet, the car will slide off the road if it is fitted with dry weather 'slick' tyres.

If the track is dry, wet weather tyres will be too slow and overheat.

Tyre choice is made by the driver. It depends on what they feel when driving the car. The decision is also helped by information from the team about what other drivers are doing.

Making the right tyre choice is often the difference between winning and losing a race.

In the 2021 Russian Grand Prix, **Lando Norris**

started from pole position and led the race in his McLaren. Lewis Hamilton was in fifth place. The track was dry. Both drivers were on 'slicks'. This was the correct choice.

A few laps from the end, Hamilton had moved into second place. Norris continued to lead. It looked like he was about to score his first Grand Prix win!

Then rain began to fall. It was not heavy at first but Hamilton decided to make a pit stop and change to **wet weather tyres.**

But Norris stayed out on slicks, hoping the track would stay dry enough to let him win the race without having to stop. It was the wrong decision.

The rain quickly became heavy. Norris's McLaren slid off the road. Lewis came through to win.

It was his **100th Grand Prix win!**

Lando eventually finished seventh. But he could have won.

SCREEEECH

ENGINEERING A WIN

Engineers do not just **design** the car. A driver works closely with their engineer at all times during a race.

They discuss how to make the car **as fast as possible** on each circuit.

During the race, the engineer keeps the driver informed by radio about what's going on around the track.

The driver is only aware of what is happening around them. They can only see the car in front and the one behind.

The engineer, watching from the pits, **sees the bigger picture.** In the same way that a football manager signals and shouts to their players from the sidelines of the pitch, the engineer talks to his driver by radio throughout the race. They discuss tactics and talk about what the other drivers are doing.

Hamilton's current race engineer is Peter Bonnington – a racing legend in his own right!

The engineer is fed information by computer. This can predict how the race is going to go. The computer can tell how the driver's tyres are likely to perform.

The engineer can also see what the opposition is doing. He can tell the driver the best time to make a pit stop and change tyres.

The engineer can see the **weather radar.** He can warn his driver that rain is coming and be prepared for the track to become wet and slippery.

The driver and the engineer can decide when the best time might be to stop and change to wet weather tyres.

Or, if it's wet, the engineer can tell the driver when other drivers are stopping to change to dry weather 'slick' tyres.

When the driver crosses the line in first place, the engineer is the first person to congratulate them on the radio!

The driver will thank the engineer. They have chosen the best strategy between them.

It's a team effort!

CLASSIC CARS

Lewis Hamilton owns a lot of cars. His garage looks more like a car park! He has been lucky enough to own several **classic cars.**

His favourite is the **Shelby Cobra.** The two-seater sports car is a beautiful beast from 1966.

The Shelby Cobra originated from a British sports car, the **AC Ace,** built in England.

When the American racing driver, **Carroll Shelby,** saw this car, he changed the small British engine for a massive **Ford V8** and renamed it **AC Cobra.** The Ford V8 has eight cylinders, four on each side in the shape of a V. Eight cylinders means lots of power!

He strengthened the car and added larger wheels to cope with the enormous power of the American engine.

The Ford V8 engine was a massive seven litres. It's **seven times the power** of the original engine in the AC Ace.

The Shelby Cobra raced at **Le Mans** and quickly became a classic. It looked and sounded incredible with its **booming exhaust pipes** on either side of the sports car.

Lewis found an example in California. Carroll Shelby himself verified that this was one of the best restored Shelby Cobras he had ever seen.

It has pride of place in Lewis's collection and does not go out on the road. It's too valuable a car to actually be driven!

Lewis bought himself a second Shelby Cobra to use on the road. He likes the car that much!

What's your favourite car? If you had unlimited money, which five cars would you put in your collection?

A LEGENDARY RIVALRY

The 2021 World Championship was turning into a **big battle** between Lewis Hamilton and **Max Verstappen** when they reached the Brazilian Grand Prix at Interlagos.

Verstappen started his Red Bull from the front row. Hamilton was all the way back in 10th place on the grid. It looked like a very tough task for Lewis to catch and pass his great rival.

The Interlagos circuit is one of the shortest in F1. It is very **tight** and **twisty** with some **steep climbs** and **big drops.**

Verstappen jumped into the lead – but Hamilton made up four places on the first lap! He is a **master at overtaking.**

By the third lap, Lewis was **fourth.**

Two laps later, he was **third.**

By lap 20, Lewis was **second** and closing in slowly on Max.

There was nothing to choose between them.

Both drivers made pit stops for fresh tyres without losing position. The smallest mistake by mechanics could have cost their driver a place. Pressure!

Verstappen countered every move by Hamilton to keep the lead.

A couple of times, Lewis got alongside Max. It was **incredibly close!** But Max just about managed to stay in front.

With just 10 laps to go, Hamilton **took the lead!**

Verstappen gave chase . . .

. . . and was close to overtaking . . .

WHO

But Hamilton held on and made it his **101st Grand Prix win!** It was another amazing drive. Very few drivers could make it from 10th place to 1st so quickly.

HAMILTON'S HEROES

Lewis has been a long-time admirer of tennis legend **Serena Williams.** They have been good friends for many years.

'I take a lot of inspiration from watching other athletes,' said Lewis. 'Serena is one of them. Seeing the way Serena has been through some hard times and pulled herself back up and had some great performances – that's been an inspiration for me.'

Serena Williams is one of the **greatest tennis players of all time.** The American has been ranked as No. 1 in the world. She has **won 23 Grand Slam titles.** That makes Lewis's record of championships look small!

Serena Williams goes regularly to Grands Prix to watch Lewis race.

Serena, like Lewis, has been active in charity work and works hard for underprivileged children in sport. She also shares Lewis's interest in fashion and music.

Together they've helped to improve world sport, raising the bar for their competitors but also opening their sports up for the next generation.

COLLECTING CARS

Lewis has always been fascinated by fast cars. He's owned quite a few!

Lewis's first road car was a Mini Cooper. As soon as he could afford it, Lewis swapped the Mini for a **Ferrari.** What a trade up!

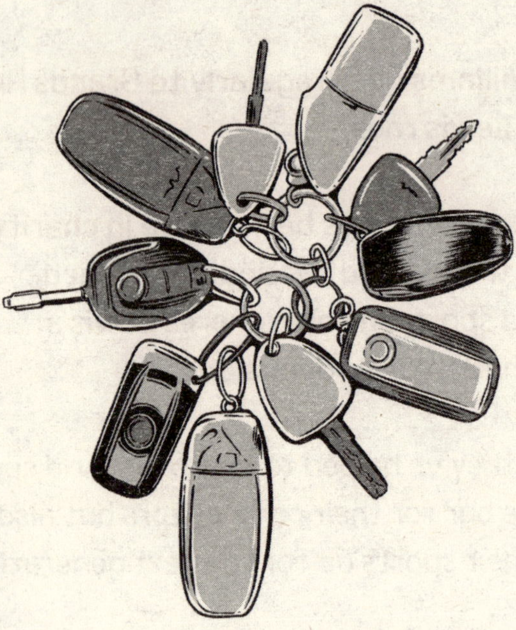

Then followed other exotic sports cars, including a £1.6m **Pagani Zonda,** more Ferraris, a **McLaren F1** and a **Mercedes AMG One.** He has also a **Cadillac,** a great American classic name in cars.

He has a **599 SA Aperta,** one of only eighty ever made.

The Mercedes AMG One has the latest state of the art hybrid turbo and electric powertrain – like his Mercedes AMG F1 car!

Lewis loves his collection of **fifteen cars** which are kept in his garages in either Monaco or Los Angeles.

'These are my art pieces,' says Lewis. 'I know a lot about cars. I'm very particular about my choice of cars. I've worked very hard for them!'

THE DANGERS OF DRIVING

Lewis Hamilton had one of his **worst-ever accidents** during his first season of F1.

It was during qualifying for the European Grand Prix at the **Nürburgring** in Germany.

A front wheel nut had not been tightened properly before Lewis left the pits to start a fast lap. The problem had been caused by a faulty wheel gun.

Lewis didn't know anything about this until he tried to turn into a left-hand corner at 240 kmh (149 mph). A front wheel came loose and the tyre punctured. Lewis completely lost control. There was nothing he could do.

The McLaren went straight on and slammed into a tyre barrier. Lewis saw it coming but could only brace himself and hope for the best.

The impact with the tyre wall took his breath away and hurt his legs badly. But thankfully, nothing was broken.

'It was one of the most painful crashes I've ever had,' said Lewis. 'My chest and my legs felt it. My head came forward and hit my chest.'

Lewis got himself out of the car. When he tried to stand up, he fell over.

After a full check up at the circuit medical centre, Lewis was flown by helicopter to hospital.

After a thorough examination, Lewis was fit enough to race the next day. He was stiff and sore. But he finished the race and scored points.

Lewis has been **racing for nearly 30 years.** Driving fast in thousands of races, he has

SCREE

managed to only have very few accidents.

His first accident happened as he started racing karts.

He was practising at a circuit called Rye House, not far from where he lived.

Another driver tried to overtake and touched Lewis's kart. It sent Lewis into a tyre wall at high speed.

The kart was badly damaged. Lewis had a nose bleed. Apart from the shock of his first accident, Lewis was okay.

Lewis's father repaired the kart and Lewis was ready to race the following day.

Lewis had an incident at Monaco during the F3 race in 2005. He touched the wall and damaged the car's suspension – but managed to keep going and win the race! That's like winning a marathon with an injured foot!

THE MONTREAL GRAND PRIX

The Montreal Grand Prix track is like no other F1 race circuit in the world.

It is on an island in the middle of the St Lawrence River, which flows past the city of Montreal.

The circuit is flat, but in a picturesque setting with water all around.

Did you know, there is a large lake on the island which was used for the rowing races during the 1976 Olympic Games?

The first Canadian Grand Prix was held on this track in 1978. The race was won by **Gilles Villeneuve,** who was Canadian.

When Villeneuve was sadly killed during practice for the 1982 Belgian GP, the track in Montreal was named **Circuit Gilles Villeneuve** in honour of the Canadian hero.

The circuit is bumpy and fast in places, with concrete walls very close. It is a very demanding track and a challenge for the drivers.

The Montreal track attracts a huge number of motor racing fans. The atmosphere is always buzzy and exciting! The only way for fans to travel to the island circuit from the city is by Metro (an underground railway).

The F1 teams and race fans enjoy the nightlife in Montreal. The Canadian Grand Prix is one of the highlights of the year.

It's safe to say it's one of Lewis's favourite tracks. He has won in Montreal **seven times.**

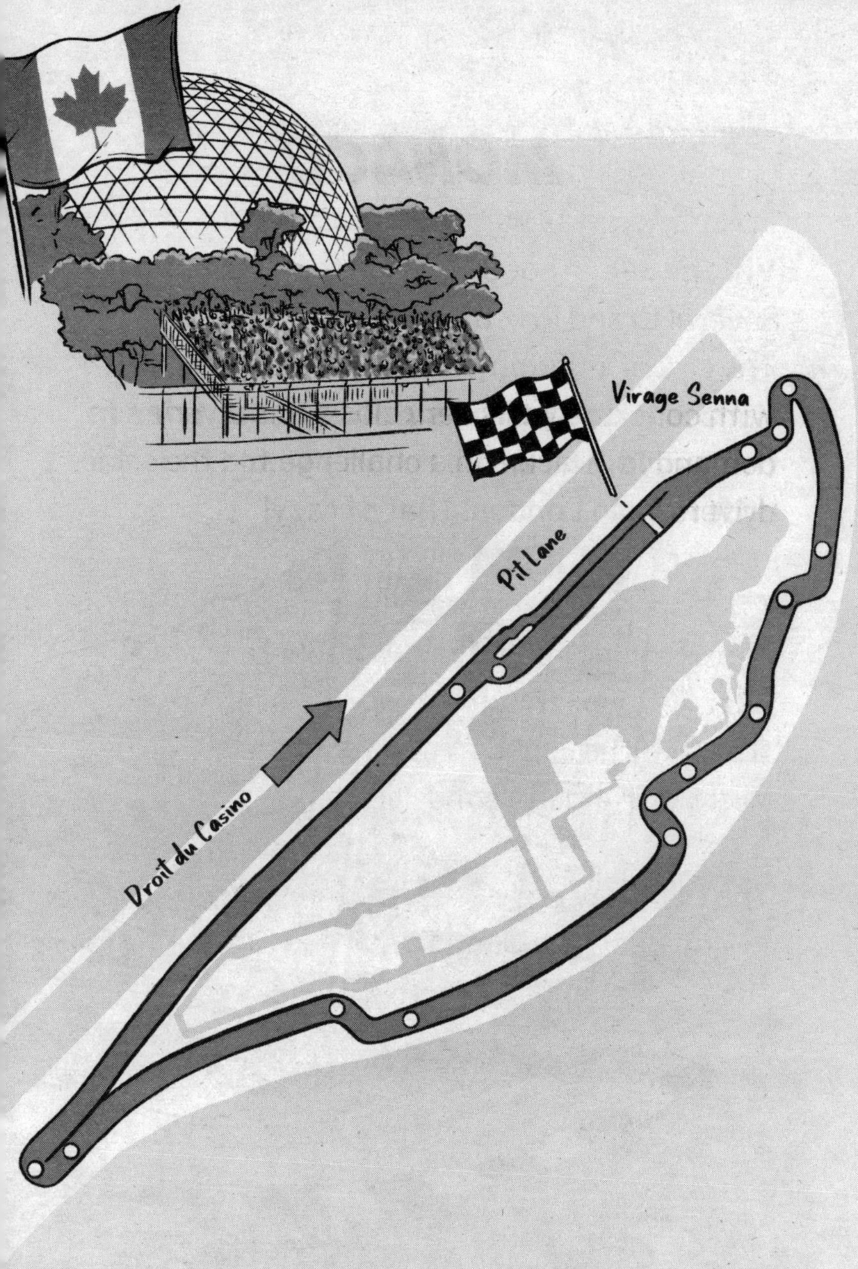

Virage Senna
Pit Lane
Droit du Casino

MONACO

Several Grand Prix drivers live in Monaco.

Monaco is **one of the smallest countries in the world.** The entire country would fit inside Hyde Park in London. That's crazy!

Monaco has low taxes, which means it is popular with Grand Prix drivers who are paid very well.

It is a beautiful place to live with a glittering harbour full of very expensive boats and yachts.

The Royal Palace is on top of a rock face, overlooking Monaco.

Ayrton Senna won six times in ten races in Monaco. No one else has beaten his record for Monaco GP wins!

Drivers do not spend much time in Monaco because they are travelling so often to the races. They keep their private planes at Nice airport, which is 20 minutes away by helicopter.

Monaco is famous for being clean and tidy. Because it is small, everything is convenient for the drivers. They enjoy the mild climate, especially in winter.

Once a year, the entire world of F1 looks to Monaco as they host their famous Grand Prix. It's always **one of the biggest racing events of the year!**

THE INDY 500

The Indianapolis 500-Mile race is known as the Indy 500.

It is **the most important motor race in the United States.** The Indy 500 has been running for more than 100 years.

The main difference between this race and a Grand Prix is that the Indy 500 is held on an oval racetrack with just four left-hand bends.

The track is known as the Indianapolis Motor Speedway. One lap measures 4 km (2.5 miles).

The Indy 500 **requires a different skillset** from drivers who go flat out all the way round each lap. They reach speeds of 370 kmh (230 mph). That's VERY fast!

There are pit stops for fuel and tyres.

VAROOOM
VAROOOOM
VAROOOM

The Indy 500 is held at the end of May each year and is often on the same weekend as the **Monaco Grand Prix.** That makes it a hugely important time of year for racing fans around the world!

Formula 1 drivers have taken part in the Indy 500 and have won the Indy 500 several times, starting with **Jim Clark,** the F1 World Champion in 1963 and 1965.

The record for most Indy 500 wins is shared between Hélio Castroneves, A. J. Foyt, Rick Mears, and Al Unser. They've won the race four times each!

The Indy 500 counted towards the F1 World Championship in the 1960s. The Indy 500 was dropped from the F1 World Championship because the race is so different and requires different types of cars.

The Indianapolis Motor Speedway has massive grandstands and seats more than 250,000 race fans each year. This produces a fantastic atmosphere!

Which race would you pick to watch, the Indy 500 or the Monaco Grand Prix?

A QUICK GUIDE TO AERODYNAMICS

When you run really fast, does it ever feel like you can feel wind in your face? This is called **air resistance.** And air resistance is actually slowing you down. It makes only a small difference when you're running, but when you're racing at hundreds of miles per hour, air resistance can make or break a race.

An F1 car is shaped this way to allow the air to pass over it as smoothly as possible. The smoother the air passes over the car, the faster it will be able to go.

The F1 car's shape helps the air pass in a certain direction. Keeping the flow of air

smooth is known as **streamlining.**

If the air does not pass over the car smoothly, it causes what is known as **drag.** Drag will slow down the car too much when it is travelling in a straight line.

When a car is going fast, it punches a hole through the air. If another car is following closely, it benefits from having the air cleared out of the way by the car in front. This means that the second car can go faster, catch up and maybe pass the car in front. This is known as **slipstreaming.**

Slipstreaming is an important tactic on the racetrack, it's a way to use the rules of aerodynamics in your favour.

An F1 car needs help when cornering. It needs the air passing over it to help push the car onto the track. This is helped by the wings on the front and back of the car. They help force the car onto the ground so that it can corner faster.

BEYOND RACING

Lewis is a big advocate for **Human Rights.**

He is not afraid to use his position as a global sports star to speak out about issues that concern him.

Lewis is **a strong supporter of the LGBTQ community.** He will make his views known when racing in countries he believes have a poor record when it comes to treating people fairly. When he races in countries that treat LGBTQ+ people badly, he wears a rainbow helmet to draw viewers' attention to this. It's a small gesture, but as Hamilton is watched by thousands of people around the world, it's an important one.

He is also a passionate believer in **Animal Rights.** He has discussed this at conferences worldwide and supports charities against illegal wildlife trade. In January 2020, Lewis

donated $500,000 to a variety of causes helping animals caught up in bushfires in Australia.

Lewis became a **vegan** to support a healthier life. Did you know he runs a vegan restaurant called Neat Burger?

Lewis is **against the use of plastics,** which

are bad for the environment. He has worked closely with the Mercedes F1 team to limit – and eliminate where possible – the use of plastic in motor-sport. 'I want everything to be recyclable,' he says. 'That includes everything from deodorant to toothbrushes.'

By helping people, animals and the environment, Lewis has proved that he wants to use his platform as a world-famous athlete for good.

HAMILTON'S HEROES

When he was seventeen, **Anthony Hamilton,** Lewis's dad, got a job as a clerk with British Rail.

He did a night school course in computing while he was working to get a better job with the railways.

Anthony took on as much extra part-time work as he could to help pay for Lewis's karting. One of the jobs was putting up signs for estate agents.

Anthony was always looking for ways to promote Lewis. He wrote to 'Blue Peter', the BBC children's TV programme, and persuaded them to film Lewis racing his radio-controlled car. So Lewis was on TV **as young as six!**

To make sure Lewis worked hard at school, Anthony would only take Lewis to the model car club if he had good reports from his school teacher. Lewis made sure that he tried extra hard in lessons – and didn't miss out on any of the fun!

When his boss would not give Lewis's dad time off to take Lewis to a kart race in Scotland, he quit his job. Anthony started his own computer company – which became very successful – and he had time to go racing with Lewis!

Anthony would work hard, persuading companies to support Lewis. This allowed Lewis to focus totally on driving. His dad would worry about finding the money to go racing.

'We are a family team,' says Lewis. 'My dad has been the motivator and the strength that kept us all going in the early days.'

LEAVING A LEGACY

Lewis Hamilton is one of the greatest examples that a sporting legend can **come from anywhere in the world** and **from any kind of background.** He proves that anyone with enough talent and enough drive can achieve their dreams.

He was bullied in school. But he did not allow

that to change his focus to be the best.

Lewis quickly became famous worldwide. But he never forgot how difficult it had been to make his way and promised to help other young people succeed.

He remained popular in motor racing because he is polite, always smiling and quietly confident. You don't need to boast when your achievements speak for themselves.

And his achievements on the racetrack have been truly incredible.

Winning a Grand Prix in his first season.

Becoming World Champion in his second season.

Winning seven World Championships.

Winning more Grands Prix than any other driver.

He is still competitive and hungry to win after **seventeen seasons as a top F1 driver.** Almost no one else has managed that in the history of the sport!

He works tirelessly for charity and to make the world a better place.

Lewis Hamilton is a **brilliant role model** – not just in F1, but in world sport in general.

Lewis Hamilton has won so many trophies – **at least a couple of hundred!** – that he doesn't have enough room for them in his home!

Lewis's father keeps some of his early trophies. Lewis prefers to keep his home free from motor racing bits and pieces.

Many of the trophies are kept by the teams he's racing for. Other trophies are kept in storage.

Lewis plans to one day have a small museum where his trophies would be on show.

Many of the trophies are reminders of proud moments. Winning his first GP in Canada in 2007. A brilliant win at Silverstone in 2008. His first karting championship in 1995.

One thing Lewis does like to keep are his crash helmets! 'They are very personal,' says Lewis. 'They're a reminder of the blood, sweat and tears that I've put into my motor racing!'

GET INVOLVED IN RACING

Many racing legends, like Lewis Hamilton, begin their careers in karting. The great thing is that it's getting easier and easier to get involved in karting, at any age! Maybe there's a track near you.

Some are small and indoors. Others are outside and look like mini-Grand Prix tracks!

To find a track near you that suits you, ask a grown-up to look online.

You can try driving a kart for a few laps and see how you get on.

If you want to race, there is plenty of advice available online about how to get started and where to buy anything from overalls and a crash helmet to finding a second-hand kart.

You can join one of the many karting clubs. They arrange races. You can race against other drivers making a start in karting. Then who knows, you could progress just like Lewis did and become the next . . .

RACING LEGEND!

VROOOM

ABOUT THE AUTHOR

Maurice Hamilton, the award-winning author of more than **thirty books** about motor-sport, has attended over **500 Grands Prix** around the world. He has been a commentator on F1 races for BBC Radio 5 Live for **20 years,** and has written about F1 for newspapers and magazines **worldwide** for decades.

ABOUT THE ILLUSTRATOR

Combining her love of **comics** with a passion for **social equality, Cat Sims** has pursued her dream career as an **artist** and **illustrator** for the past decade. She has worked on a huge range of commercial and personal projects for clients including *The New Yorker*, *Jacobin*, Adidas, the BBC and many more.
www.catsims.org / @cat_sims